Do You Know How Kind I Am?

Kathleen Bell

Leafe Press

Published by Leafe Press
Nottingham, England.
www.leafepresspoetry.com

Cover photograph by Kathleen Bell

ISBN: 978-1-9999451-7-6

Do You Know How Kind I Am?

1.

Out there's a woman, driving a bus.
Her only cargo is cloth, metal and air
and at night, light.

Out there's a man who walks dutiful, slow,
lugging a bag.
Two talk at a distance – a third
leans in to listen.
The masked and gloved make their way
into shops. Some stumble at kerbs.

Others are sniffing the air
as if free but they know
it may hold disaster and death
and breath can bring pain in its train.

2.

We noticed war,
observed the fire.
We watch for flood.
And now it's come –
the great sickness.

3.

Take the test (but there are no tests).
Wear the mask (and make it yourself
                    – where is the needle and thread?)
We are locked down. Our minds scurry
like mice trapped, wanting food, wanting treats
 and the promise that one day
 life will be well.

4.

No-one's had it – not that I know –
no-one that matters. Well, there's my cleaner,
her father too, but they were overweight –
almost obese, they could have joined a gym
or jogged to work – they could have been just fine
but weren't. It's underlying health –
that's what they'll say, I'm pretty sure
and we can't know for certain
not that it was, well, Covid, it was early on
before the testing. Like I say,
no-one I know but now I need a cleaner –
somebody quiet, healthy, who social distances
and comes to work in a mask, ideally,
lives on her own – to cut the risk
but like I say, it's not much
more than a cold and no-one has had it,
no-one I know, no-one I really know.

5.

There's the plain mask,
the paisley-patterned,
the clearly home-made
from T-shirt or tea-towel,
the old scarf coiled round the face,
the silk square worn as bandana,
the pale blue, not-quite-see-transparent throw-away mask
(drop after wearing, float it in puddle or gutter)
the cat-face, dog-face, lion-face, death's head,
artistic mask that flatters,
the made-to-order
or clan tartan,
the mask of your face
with beard that's plainly fake.

6.

Squeeze your eyes
though your face swelters.
Maybe you'll show
acknowledgement
or thanks, or regret
at the loss of a world
no longer ours.

7.

Who dares interrogate
the bare face
or risk the eruption of trauma?
We must stay alert

to unseen damage: the hurt body,
the scarred mind, the unsettled soul.
This venture to the station
is at some risk

not just of sickness
but the vivid threat:
and angry screech
spat into face.

I'm watching those who work.
Thank you, I say
and wonder, do they know
how kind I am?

8.

When you come to clean
keep your breath to yourself.
Mask at all times.
I'll be there, checking up.

Me? Wear a mask? Why should I
in my own home? – It's just me
while you are working.
There'll be no-one here.

9.

Each friend is confined
to a box on a screen
but they all raise a glass and pretend
the world is unchanged, then say
"when this is over" and mention
their broken plans.

There's enough grief for the big things
we can't control, so it all spills out
in little furies: a daytrip's deferred,
a holiday lost, a meeting missed,
a gig postponed
(and sometimes we say this
claiming we're sorry mostly for those
who lost their work and we list them:
the holiday crew, the chefs, performers denied
the gift of our joy, our applause ,
our thanks, and their wish to perform).

When time comes
for separate space outdoors,
for picnics, pictures to share
on Instagram, on Facebook,
let us pretend
that this new normal
is the old normal.
Then we can celebrate
each small advance,
and still stay distant from our friends
for one another's sake.

10.

and the big question is
       who will we call to sacrifice themselves?
       who, if it comes to that, will we choose to desert
       untreated, strangled
       by the breath that will not come?

11.

We think of what it's like
to be aspirated, stuck to a machine
that does our breathing for us,
spits in our airways, forces our lungs
inward and outward, filters the air
and we think of what it's like
when plastic-faced strangers
touch us with plastic hands, when voices
arrive like a voice underwater
through mask, computer or phone
and do their best to assure us, remotely,
that no-one is really alone.

12.

I calculate risk and am glad
I'm not an old man a bit overweight
with a murmuring heart, whose cousins
are still in Bangladesh though he's lived here
all of his life, shares a home
with his daughters, and one is a carer
who works with dementia, the other
(he's sad to say it but loves her) a single mum –
her two small boys are his joy.
He's not that old, he can still drive a cab.
He dreamt of being a lawyer – that wasn't to be
but he won't complain, the boys have a future
so now, to help them out, he finds spare time
to work at the corner shop,
where he serves and does the accounts,
and as a good neighbour he helps the infirm
with mending and shopping and getting to mosque ...
but I'm glad I'm not him, even though
he speaks four languages, is greatly loved
by family and friends, does useful work and knows
that he's high risk, but takes that risk
daily for others' good and for
the family he loves.

13.

Bandage my heart
from hurt
and deepening care
and keep grief far from my door.

14.

Those who flee bombings,
flood, fire, earthquake,
the empty ache in a belly,
and those who want food for their children,
or hope, or a better life
must all be imprisoned
to keep us safe.
We must send them back
to wherever they came from,
those bearers of plague
who must take it back
to wherever they came from.
The world is peopled
by too many folk.

15.

Organise, please
one dead celeb a week
or, if you can't, somebody blonde,
pretty of course, and young
in floods of tears, for failing that
how can we hope
to unite a nation's grief?

16.

Let's tell it all as a story
and if there's a story
there must be a villain
and if there's a villain
there must be a hero
and if there's a plot it's a puzzle
and there to be solved
so somebody sees it straight
and it must be you

but the people are sheep
and the powers are liars
and everything's false
and we're all fooled –
all of us, all of the time –
except you

and the trouble is, we know
that governments lie,
conspiracies happen,
and sometimes we want to believe
in raging rebels
declaiming truth
against the truth of our eyes.
We're all in a lockdown
so how can we know?

Where have they gone,
the ones we saw, the rough sleepers,
the troubled and angry
who scrawled upon cardboard and walls
or yelled into phones?
Do they really sleep in hotels?
Were they taken to centres for testing
and cared for softly
or rounded up into camps,
or swept into alien ships?

In separate homes
we can't unpick the truth
and only your tale
(the one we don't believe)
offers the ending we want.

17.

The borders close and tighten
with checkpoints,
surveillance.

Meanwhile   air
                    glides
bearing who knows what droplets

over a fence, under a gate,
skimming lake, road, sea
into streets, fields, a home

where, like breath,
it rises
and enters breath

and becomes breath

18.

It's not real, you know, the virus.
It's them. I wouldn't say it
– I'm not on his side – but this time
Trump speaks the truth. It's Deep State
and Black Lives Matter – they're in it together,
they want us masked, applauding and kneeling –
it's all about control, can't you see?
And look at all those sheeple, muzzled,
staying apart (so bad for the kids), just doing
whatever they're told. I said to her
"I won't go into your shop, at any price,
if you force me to muzzle." You've got to show them
you're not afraid. So why don't you
come out, bring all your friends, dance in the streets?
Imagine the world that we'd make if we all said "No."
Then children could cuddle their friends, and teachers
would tell them the truth, about Deep State
and government lies. They kill you, you know,
in the National Horror Service, to keep up the deaths
though the figures aren't real, they make them all up –
you can see if you count for yourself.
Anyway, there was my aunt – my friend's aunt –
OK, I don't know her – the friend of a friend –
she'd flu, just usual flu, they said it was Covid. Not true.
She had a stroke, the way people do, and would have got well
but suddenly died and they wrote – the nurses –
"Covid" on all the forms. The family
said it was wrong, she shouldn't have died.
Suspicious, no? But it's all Clap for the Carers
and Save NHS and why can't everyone see
that it's all a lie? Those nurses on telly –
they're not real. Those doctors – they're just
crisis actors, my friend says, government puts them there
and it's not just them, it's royals, the banks

and their paedo plan which they're covering up
and they want us all subdued – but I won't be,
I'm in the Resistance – because they're ready
to take your kids, and vaccinate you
for something that doesn't exist. There's no vaccinations,
it's something to make you obey. And why do you think
they call it "Track and Trace" – they want to know
exactly where you are. And everyone's in it:
Bill Gates, the Clintons, Soros, the Dalai Lama,
Blair, Colin Kaepernick, Masons, the Pope,
Quakers, the BBC, and teachers (with some exceptions),
and Nelson Mandela (who's not really dead),
the Queen, Prince Philip – they're lizards really,
you see it in their eyes, they'd all be dead
if this thing were real. So listen –
I'm checking Facebook, although it covers up
most of the truth, and there's good stuff
on the Dark Web. I'm checking it now.
I'll be back soon with more proof.
Just watch – I'll let you know.

19.

I learnt to name
cocksfoot
rye grass
meadow fescue

        Food bank queues
        stretch along pavements,
        chill hands
        turn the heating down

One day I saw
great spotted woodpecker
blackcap
kestrel

        City bins
        are empty of food.
        Sleepers in alleys
        lack passers-by

In dreams
I crest waves,
salt crystals encrust me:
I float, secure

        Adrift, there's only
           one child's bucket
           to sweep entire seas,
           from a crowded craft.

20.

Polish the glass between us and the world.
Let the routine of grief
play itself out on a screen
                and when time permits
                    we'll glance
from our distanced lives,
careful, enclosed.